T0195014

OVERCOMING

PERSONAL JOURNEY OF COURAGE

DOKK ELLE, TH.D.

OVERCOMING
PERSONAL JOURNEY OF COURAGE

iUniverse books may be ordered through booksellers or by contacting:

iUniverse
1663 Liberty Drive
Bloomington, IN 47403
www.iuniverse.com
844-349-9409

ISBN: 978-1-6632-3879-5 (sc)
ISBN: 978-1-6632-3881-8 (hc)
ISBN: 978-1-6632-3880-1 (e)

Library of Congress Control Number: 2022907577

Print information available on the last page.

iUniverse rev. date: 05/25/2022

CONTENTS

ACKNOWLEDGEMENTS

My warmest thanks to my awesome, assistant editor and supportive spouse, Patrice L., my mother, Nancy Mae Dunbar, my dad, Edward "Jack" Stroman, my stepdad, Joseph "Tojo" Smith, my awesome young adult children Courtney A. and Benjamin I. You continuously inspired me to be all that I was born to be in the Trinity. Your untiring love, support, encouragement and inspiration has propelled me to reach beyond the break in order to achieve another milestone. You often reminded me to never give up and never quit for being mindful that other souls are depending on me to be an over achiever in numerous aspects of life. Thanks for your positive energy, wisdom, knowledge, understanding, thoughts and ideas while writing this first (book) of many series. Thanks, in a million ways, while I'm forever grateful for all that you are to me and a reminder of what I could achieve.

1

The Beginning of Life
as I Knew It

*W*hew! This sun is hot on my back! It feels like it's 120 degrees, and there's no shade to be found! This South Carolina heat is no joke! I can see the heat rise over the field. I feel like I'm drowning in my own sweat! My mouth is as dry as cotton, and my stomach keeps growling to remind me that it's already time to eat. But I can't eat yet. I must wait until we're almost done working. Plus, I must wait for my mother to finally split that small amount of bologna and cornbread among me and my siblings.

Why do I have to be out here in this big field picking cotton! Cotton! I see it far and wide—nothing but white blooms of it. And the thorns don't help either! I've probably cut myself twenty times already. Maybe I can get Grandma to wrap some strips of cloth around my fingers to avoid getting all *those deep cuts. She wraps her hands like that. This field must be the length of three or four football fields! I'm only eight years old! It's Saturday! I should be plopped down in front of the TV watching cartoons or a good western! But no, I must be out in this scorching heat helping my mother pick this darn cotton, only to find out that we're only going to get a few measly dollars for all of our hard work. I can't believe that we're out here picking cotton as if we're living back in slavery times! Why can't I just be a kid and not worry about helping my family earn money to live? I may be young, but I already know that this is not what I want to do forever. There has to be a better way, and I'm going to find out what that way might be. I don't want this to be all there is to my life. I must find something else to do that doesn't require this hard work in the hot sun. Yeah, I must find myself. But how can I?*

When I was a young lad, I realized that I was to do special things in life. First, I had to find out what life was all about and who I really was. I also had to discover the ultimate reason for my existence. Why had I been born? What was my purpose in life? I thought this would be a challenging task. Well, in order to even begin to figure out what my purpose in life was, I must start from the beginning. I was born with the name Larry Seawright[1] in the late 1950s in Jamaica Queens, New York, in Queens General Hospital. My mother is Nancy Mae Seawright, and my father is Edward (Jack) M. Stroman. My mother made numerous trips from New York to South Carolina to visit my grandmother, who was said to be sickly many times. So my mother would travel back and forth between the two states to attend to her sickly mother, and at some time during her traveling, she gave birth to me in New York. There became a time when my mother would

---

[1] This is the life and times of the person formerly known as Dr. Larry Seawright, now known as Dr. Dokk Elle. The name Seawright could never make me who God has made me to be. I refuse to give any allegiance to the name but have taken on my own God-given identity. Stay tuned for the reasons behind the name change.

make her last trip between South Carolina and New York. So I primarily grew up in South Carolina.

In my first memory of myself being in existence, I was about four or five years old. I was the fifth child out of eleven born into the family. Initially, I just played around the house with my siblings, neighbors, and friends until around the age of five or so. I did not have a care or concern in the world at that juncture. This thing called life was all a mystery to me.

I didn't understand much at all and was totally dependent upon my mother as my teacher and sole provider. To my knowledge and memory, my mother never worked what some people would call "public job." So along with my grandmother, myself, and my siblings, my mom earned a "living" by picking cotton, fruits, and vegetables in the fields of our town. Yes! Picking cotton! In the 1950s and 60s! It's *still* hard to believe that my mother picked cotton just over five decades ago, not five *centuries* ago! You must understand that our little town and surrounding areas were mainly agricultural with some factories that hired local people. But she did the best job that she could with what she had.

So, I began life as I knew it without indoor plumbing or electricity and with limited finances. Initially, and for many years to come, we didn't receive any state, county, or federal assistance from the government, although we had low income or practically no income at any given time. I'm sure many others drew this type of assistance. Although we were less fortunate, we were in the dark about how to get assistance. Why couldn't someone had told us about the help that was available to less-fortunate families? This is one of the very reasons that I make it my mission to always give back to my mother and community. We must all look out for our families, friends, and neighbors. It's the kindest thing to do.

We just had to survive the best way that we knew. Rather,

my mother had to provide for and raise all eight of us children with the bare minimum. She and my grandmother worked the landlords' fields to earn enough money to pay rent on their shacks. When my mother was not earning a living picking cotton or harvesting crops by hand for low wages, she occasionally earned extra cash by housekeeping and babysitting for Ms. Diane, a Caucasian woman who lived on the other side of the railroad tracks that divided the town. She earned only fifteen dollars per week and, at times, had to secure a babysitter for us children when she couldn't see us off to school or welcome us home after school. Mother paid her grandmother (my great-grandmother), whom we called Granny, half of her of weekly earnings. Yes, believe it or not, but it's true that we survived, for the most part, on only thirty dollars a month for years! I don't recall having a male role model or father figure early on in my life (not even her husband was around—more to follow on him). So, I knew only to look to my mother for all things that I needed to survive. I never noticed any negligence on my mother's part when it came to raising and taking care of us.

I also remembered that, at this early point in time, I didn't see my grandmother on my mother's side very much either. I have very vivid memories of her as well. I just remembered the feeling that my grandmother was not always, if ever, incredibly supportive toward my mother, her one and only daughter. So, my mother has always felt a certain way about seeing the need to make herself available and supportive to my grandmother's needs as she expected. My mother would often, until recently, mention this to my siblings and me. She sounded upset or even disappointed in how she may have missed out on certain things in life by making the sacrifices to attend to my grandmother's needs. It's important to note that my mother and grandmother didn't exactly have a huge gap in age. Anyone who didn't know any better would've thought they were sisters. Throughout the years, I often wondered why my grandmother needed my mother's help so much and so often. I'm unable to recall that my mother would have any disputes with my grandmother; neither would my mother ever push back or disrespect my grandmother. Instead, she would just take all things into account and keep it moving forward.

At this time, we lived in a shack that was located off a long dirt road right outside of town. Soon thereafter, in the little town of Salley, South Carolina, I attended school at Sardis Elementary School. I started school in the first grade because we didn't have pre–kindergarten or kindergarten at that time.

Since we didn't have electricity in some of the places we eventually lived, we didn't have an alarm clock. We had to rely on God, His angels, and my mother to awake us somehow. In the few places we lived during my early childhood, my siblings and I would sometimes miss the school bus because we overslept and felt too cold to get out of bed. I recall my siblings and I walking and sometimes running through the woods to get to school.

When my mother was unable to see us off to school and be at home when we came home, she would gather us for a ride to Granny's house before she went off to work. Granny would only ensure that we got off to school in a timely manner, and then we would return to her house after school. From Granny's house, we would walk only two to three hundred yards down the street to Sardis Elementary School. Granny would seldom feed us anything, not even a snack, but she cooked for those who lived with her. I remember thinking that something seemed wrong about not being fed anything most times while in Granny's "care." At the time, we didn't understand what I now know as neglect.

At the time, even at such an early age, I realized that there were some reasons that she charged my mother half of her weekly income for watching us for a few hours most days and getting us off to that short walk to school. I just remember feeling that it just didn't seem right or fair for Granny to take half of what my mother earned just to watch us walk from her yard to the front door of the schoolhouse.

So, was my mother being cheated out of her earnings by her own grandmother and our great-grandmother? I don't remember how Granny discovered how much money my mother got paid weekly for housekeeping, but she required half of my mother's earnings. It's just hard to believe that we survived on such little money.

I often saw an evil woman who lived next door to Granny. I will refer to this person as Derd. Their houses were on the same plot of land but were separated by an ash pile. Granny and Derd didn't have a friendly or neighborly relationship at all. I didn't know who this lady was or why she was so hateful toward Granny. Derd cursed out Granny to no end. Later, I came to realize that she was Granny's own daughter! She was also my tormentor for years to come. It wasn't until many years passed that I would finally come to know why she acted this way toward her own mother and me. More to follow on her reasons for disrespecting Granny and directing her abusive behavior toward me.

Derd was my great-aunt and a hell angel who often physically, mentally, and verbally abused me. I simply just didn't know or understand why she despised me in the worst way possible. Unfortunately, it wasn't until the late 1900s that I would finally learn the truth behind Derd's abuse and negative attitude toward me. The truth is mind-blowing to say the least. Stay tuned to a future installment for the answers.

2

Getting Ready for the World and Expectations

A s I have mentioned, my family and I lived in a little wooden shack just outside of town, and we picked cotton to earn money. When I was about ten or eleven years old, as I worked in the various fields, I would give half of what I had earned for the day to my mother. I just felt this was the right thing to do at an exceedingly early age, and to this day, I still give back to my mother monetarily and in many other ways.

I believe I had an inkling from Father God that I must share my earnings and support my mother. On average, I made about four to eight dollars for a day's work, and I couldn't wait to get home and share half with my mother. It made me feel so good to know that I was giving back to my mother! We worked in the fields owned by well-to-do Caucasian townsmen. I picked cotton in what I thought were the longest of rows of any cotton field. It seemed that the cotton rows would never end. But my hardworking grandmother could pick four rows of cotton at the same time.

The old wooden shacks we lived in were just up the road from the cotton fields. Sometimes I was so frustrated over what I didn't understand about all the hard work we performed for measly wages. I used to cry whenever I saw the roads that led to those fields. Until this day, I still am emotionally affected when I see certain roads that remind me of all the times we had to go to the fields. It's almost as if I experience post-traumatic stress at even the thought of those fields.

I just wanted to sneak home and forget about working. But I don't recall ever having done so, or at least not without permission from my mother or grandmother. I didn't understand why we were giving slave labor to this white man and not being blessed enough to have our own land and work for ourselves.

3

The "Shack Lord"

W hen I was growing up, we lived in a few dwellings that were considered shacks. The only redeeming thing I can say about those shacks is that they kept us from sleeping in the elements. They provided very little shelter, but my mother and grandmother made do with what they could afford. Some had electricity, but none had indoor plumbing. Most times, we used candles and kerosene lamps for light and woodburning stoves for heat. We had to chop wood year-round. Later, we finally used propane gas. We used outhouses and gathered water from local underground springs, neighbors' houses, and the local church. Sometimes, the property had a well from which we could draw water.

We were also able to fill fifty-gallon metal drums with rainwater. That water was mainly used for washing clothes and taking baths, which we did in a basin or foot tub. I remembered living in one wooden four-room shack—no, not a four-bedroom shack. There were only four rooms in that shack!

In some parts of the house there were cracks between the floorboards, and I could see the ground from inside the house. During the winter, we would get so cold! We had to help keep each other warm the best way that we knew how. We had a couple of beds, and we all slept together. At that time, there were approximately five out of seven siblings who lived there together with my mother and me. Our grandmother always lived nearby, and although we didn't have a lot of things, we were a close-knit, loving family. Despite our living conditions and circumstances, the good Lord provided life and security for us.

The shack-lord was seemingly nice, but he wasn't nice enough to ensure that we had proper indoor plumbing in the old shacks. But he had a nice, gigantic home in the town of Salley with all essential indoor plumbing and extras. When I visited him to pay the rent, mow his lawn, or to ask general questions, I would, every time, ask permission to enter his "mansion"—a very appropriate way to describe his house in comparison to ours. I was amazed at how he was living compared to the way we were living. I liked the landlord's home so much that I would just try to stay in that nice house for as long as I could. I would just look around at the nice ceilings, walls, and furnishings and dream of someday having better conditions and more conveniences for my mother and family. But I couldn't bring myself to even think big like that early on. Neither was I able to think that it was even possible.

The struggle was too great to overcome in the meantime. While most times I felt defeated in many ways, I still tried to maintain my composure in my mother's presence and the presence of others. Yes, I always felt that I was a thinker and could somehow figure this life out, but with a lot of help from God instead of the people around me. Well, let me check back into reality. I didn't have time to waste, and I had to be back on the road in order to deliver the rent receipts to mother and grandmother for their records. There was no time to daydream about having a better life. We had to work and survive through our poor circumstances. I had many thoughts, and the main one was to hurry and grow up so I could find a better way of life and give back to my mother and grandmother.

I never understood why I was often tasked by my mother and grandmother to carry out certain responsibilities, sometimes even more frequently than my older siblings. On many occasions when food in the pantry and the refrigerator or ice box ran low, my mother would make out a food request list for me to carry to town. I would have to ask the grocery store owner to give us food on credit until my mother had the money to repay him. Boy, was I happy when he approved the grocery list for my mother?

But at other times, he wouldn't honor my mother's request, and he would tell me to relay that message to her. I would be so hurt, disappointed, and sad, but I still had to walk back a couple of miles and cross two bridges to tell my mother the bad news. I would cry over half the way back home, but I had to quickly dry up those tears.

I never complained to my mother and grandmother. This put me on a positive but challenging course of life that would someday pay great and rewarding dividends. It taught me obedience, responsibility, sacrifice, discipline, and a better understanding of what it was like to grow in all that life had to offer a little country boy.

~~~~~~~

We begin life with purpose.

Genesis 1:1–2, 26:

> In the beginning God created the heavens and the earth. Now the earth was formless and empty, darkness was over the surface of the deep, and the Spirit of God was hovering over the waters.
>
> Then God said, "Let us make mankind in our image, in our likeness, so that they may rule over the fish in the sea and the birds in the sky, over the livestock and all the wild animals, and over all the creatures that move along the ground."

1 Peter 5:6–7: "Humble yourselves, therefore, under God's mighty hand, that He may lift you up in due time. Cast all your anxiety on Him because He cares for you."

Your life started perfectly from where God planned for you to begin this journey. You are not a mistake but one who has a purpose and a reason for living. We need to present all our worries, anxieties, and problems to God in order to let Him handle them.

4

Separation and Hardships

D espite the hardships we faced at home, I always enjoyed going to school. It was an escape from having to work as a young child in cotton fields to help support my family. During my second-grade year, I missed forty to fifty days of school largely due to being too ill to attend. We didn't have access to proper medical care to treat my whooping cough. That year, I had a severe bout of it. Nevertheless, when I returned to school, I immersed myself in learning.

One day, I had to stay in from recess because I didn't know the answer to a math question that my homeroom teacher, Mrs. O. asked me. My classmate, S. N., tried whispering the answer to me, but the teacher heard him and gave me a different math problem. Again, I struggled and was unable to answer. Later, I was transferred to Ms. R. W.'s class where I became so good at math that I would ante up the piece of fruit from my lunch for math competitions, and I would always win my fruit back. Math, even after high school, became my favorite subject.

5

*A Christmas to
Remember, or Not*

During the Thanksgiving and Christmas seasons, my siblings and I would set out to find a Christmas tree in the nearby woods. For a few years in a row, we found a Christmas tree to put up in the house in the hope that we would be blessed to have Santa put something under the tree for us. We would cut down a small enough pine tree and make believe that it was an actual Christmas tree. We couldn't afford to purchase one, so it was the next best thing we could find. So, the pine tree cutting lasted for a few more years and ended right before I became a teenager.

This all worked out well for me because that also was the last year I would receive toys from the Salvation Army. The Salvation Army gave poor, underprivileged children toys and other gifts during Christmas, and our family was fortunate to receive those donations. Otherwise, we wouldn't have known what it was like to have gifts to open on Christmas Day. It meant so much to all of us children. We couldn't wait until that time of year came around. Maybe twice a year we were given clothing vouchers. The sponsorship programs were run by the school's social workers. They would pick us up from home or school and take us shopping because we didn't have our own transportation.

They would always take us shopping to buy our back-to-school clothing. Once we picked out our clothing, they would hand the vouchers over to the store manager, Mr. J. M. When we found something that we liked, we would then ask Mr. J. M. about the cost, and he would always reply with a number ending in ninety-nine ($10.99, $5.99, $3.99, etc.) and that was so funny to us.

We also shopped at the locally owned department store. Once we receive our new clothes, we felt important and special for a short moment. I cried over no longer being eligible to receive any more toys because there was an age cutoff at twelve. But I got over it quickly in order to make room for my younger siblings to receive those gifts instead.

During this time, my family and I were still moving from one old shack after another, still often without indoor plumbing or running water, and sometimes without electricity. Although we didn't have proper facilities in any of the shacks that we lived in for years, my mother and grandmother still had to pay the monthly rent to landlords who lived like kings and queens. I never knew just how poor we were until I visited homes that provided all the necessities for living. There was a glaring difference between our living conditions and the people who lived in such dwellings.

6

My Missing Family

I had three sisters—M. A., S. D., and D. M.—whom either I never saw, or I even remember living with us during any of those lean years. M. A. was my oldest sister who, as an infant, died in my mother's arms during a train ride between South Carolina and New York. I was born after M. A. Through my mother, the only memory I have of her is that she died prematurely in my mother's arms. Until today, my mother still senses and is reminded of M. A.'s brief, earthly presence and death. S. D. and D. M. lived elsewhere together.

I later discovered that some nosy people reported my mother to the county department of family and children's services to complain about her not being able to raise seven children by herself, especially my two living sisters at the time—maybe because they were girls. I don't remember the exact reason for their removal from my mother's custody. The State of South Carolina, Aiken County, not only took my two sisters from my mother, but they also took the sisters away from us siblings. I am sure that my mother was hurt over not having all her children together, but she never spoke about it until we were old enough to understand better. Later, we moved to another old house that was located off a dirt road to be closer to Grandma N. J. J.'s home. While we were visiting my grandmother, some visitors showed up with my two sisters. They had adopted them through the state or county's adoption program.

We siblings didn't clearly understand why they had been separated from us, but I discovered that one of my sisters (D. M.) was okay, while it was determined that my sister S. D. couldn't walk or talk due because she had cerebral palsy. A few years later, we discovered that my two sisters had been separated from each other because their adoptive parents had aged greatly and were no longer able to care for them, although they put up a fuss over losing them *and* the monthly child support check, which was top priority to them.

When I was a teenager and was old enough to get a learner's permit and later a driver's license, I was able to afford to buy a car from one of my brothers. I would often drive my mother and grandmother to visit D. M. who was, at the time, living in another city. Her adoptive parents were very hospitable and friendly to us, but the state would only allow us to transport my sister to local area restaurants to have lunch with us. We had a strict timeline to follow and had to have her back to her adoptive parents' home by a certain time. We always honored their request. Today, D. M. lives and works in Aiken County; she is married and has children.

My sister S. D. was living in a rehabilitation home in Charleston, South Carolina, by that time. My mother and I visited her as often as possible. She remained at the rehab center until she passed away. In 1985, I called home from my army duty station at Fort Carson, Colorado, only to discover that S. D. had died and had been buried soon thereafter. I didn't learn about her death in time to attend her funeral. The loss of my sister was very painful as was the knowledge that no immediate family member sought to make any effort to contact me. Even through the loss of my sister, I knew that I had to keep journeying on with the life with which I was blessed.

7

Working Together

For the most part, I saw that we were a very close-knit family because my grandmother, my mother, my siblings, and I would go to various sites and work the fields together as one unit. Grandma always lived close to us for most of the earlier years. When I was five or six years old, and it was time for my mother to give birth to another one of my siblings, she would have us gather some clothing and quilts or blankets for the walk to Grandma's house where we would stay until she gave birth to our newest brother or sister.

My grandmother was always very loving, kind, thoughtful,

considerate, and helpful to us at all costs. She made many sacrifices for us. Neither my grandmother nor my mother ever complained even though I didn't understand why we didn't have adequate supplies or the necessary things to live a more wholesome life as did others. My mother and grandmother never explained to us why things were the way they were, so we just kept moving periodically from shack to shack, trying to survive the best way we knew how.

My grandmother, whom we also referred to as Skutt, lived in her own home and sold moonshine as another form of financial support. I don't remember my grandmother's husband, Granddaddy L. J., for he died early on, so none of us were old enough to have known him. But we were told how much he loved and spoiled my oldest brother, nicknamed June, when he was a baby. We often heard our mother and grandmother speak highly of Granddaddy L. J., saying that he was a good man.

Sometime after I started elementary school, my cousin and second-grade teacher, Floria Harris, introduced my siblings and me to our paternal grandfather, Edward Dunbar. So periodically, we would go to visit Granddaddy Edward, who lived with his sister, Aunt Margaret. Granddaddy Edward was terminally ill and bedridden. We all would gather around his bed and listen to what had he to say.

Although we enjoyed spending time with Granddaddy Edward, we never had a close, personal relationship with him. I don't recall attending his funeral. I still have pictures of him and often think about how things would have been had he been able to establish a relationship with us. I felt that he was a good, genuine man.

8

That Missing Link

To the best of my knowledge and memory, my mother always lived in Salley, South Carolina, while her husband, my stepdad, lived and worked in Jamaica, Queens, New York. I didn't understand why my eldest three siblings' dad wasn't with the family. To this day, not one word has ever been spoken about it by my mother or those siblings. I can attest to the fact that *none* of our fathers was in the household or supported our mother in any way that would ease our financial burdens.

As I recall, back in the day, children weren't allowed to be in grown folk's presence when they were conversing with each other. One memorable moment was when my great-grandmother was talking to her neighbor, and I stepped up to ask her a question. Before I could finish my question, she spit her snuff into my eyes! She never looked at me and kept talking to her friend as if I didn't exist. I felt the burning from the wad and ran inside to clear my eyes. No, the elders back then didn't put up with children listening to their conversations or being in their presence unless they were called. This was old-school discipline, and I learned a lesson that I never forgot. Sometimes it feels as if I can still feel that burning sensation in my eyes to this day! I digress.

A child didn't dare ask why a husband left his wife and children home alone permanently or why the family wasn't together any longer. Times have really changed since then. Children today feel more comfortable giving their opinions and are sometimes invited to do so or to ask questions about situations. We, as children, stayed in our place. But I couldn't help noticing for a long period of time that we were growing up without a dad or granddad in our lives.

Thank God that a man nicknamed Tojo came along at the right time in our lives. He was a real man who stepped up to the plate to shoulder the emotional and financial responsibilities that our biological fathers failed to handle. I'll "introduce" Tojo a little later.

I personally know that it is of the highest importance for a father figure—or a grandfather figure—to be present in a family. Without that positive male presence in the home and family circle, the family struggle is multiplied. The lack of that presence in our home set us up for difficult times for years. I know now from personal experience that it's extremely important to have a balance of support—physical, emotional, and financial—in every home.

I never understood why a father or grandfather was not present in our home, but I did feel that something about the makeup of our family didn't look or feel right. But still I didn't ask any questions about why our family struggled so hard and why there seemed to not be any help from our fathers. And this begs the question—why *weren't* any of our fathers around to help our mother take care of us?

I can speak for myself and a few others about the deadbeat dads who procreated children but were never forced or even required (by the mothers or the state) to support them. Well, you cannot force anyone—including your dad—to be in your life. Fathers must have a desire to do so themselves. But I've never even *thought* about having children and not being present in their lives— *at all!* In my personal experience as a father, I have physically and financially supported my children so they would never know what was like to not have the necessities of life and more. And they would never know what it would be like not to have *emotional* support as well from their father, as I never had from mine.

My mother didn't make us children by herself. So why was it okay to let her struggle like that as she took care of my siblings and me? It was a hard life that I wouldn't wish on my worst enemy. The moral of the story is that fathers must take care of their children. If they can't support them financially, then they must be there for them emotionally. Both types of care should go hand in hand and without saying. But this has been a recurring theme and fact of life for me and my siblings. I believe that, if my father had only a dollar to give to my mother, but had spent countless times with me, that it would have made a positive, lasting impression on me knowing that my father acknowledged, loved, and cared for me. Thank God that He has always been my Father despite my biological father not stepping up to the plate to make sure that I was okay. I also thank Father God that my dad's shortcomings as a father didn't prevent me from being a great father to *my* children.

The sins of the fathers don't have to visit their children. In other words, fathers today don't have to take on the same attitude as their deadbeat fathers by not acknowledging their responsibilities to their children. Our fathers had no good excuses for not taking care of us as they should have out of a sense of decency, if not legal decree.

Regardless of how we may feel or think of our parents, or how they may treat or have treated us, God still expects us to love and respect them and always show them dignity. God doesn't give us options to consider loving them or not.

Hold honor above all else.

Ephesians 6:2: "'Honor your father and mother.' This is the first commandment with a promise.

Exodus 20:12: "Honor your Father and mother, so that you may live long in the land the Lord your God is giving you.

Deuteronomy 5:1–23: Please read the Ten Commandments.

9

My Godsend, Tojo

By this time, my stepdad, Tojo, had come into my life and had made all the difference going forward. This was the nickname that I gave him as a play on his real name, Joseph. He meant a lot to me and, in short, was the father I had never had! He was so humble, caring, smart, and willing to take on a ready-made family of eight children and their mother.

I wasn't sure he had a clue about what he was taking on. But after a while, I observed that he had adjusted well and went forward with his "marching orders." His relationship with my mother was contingent upon how much he loved her, which must've been a lot, considering she had so many children. I loved Tojo and would often go into the woods with him to cut down a tree or two for fuel for cooking and heating when the propane gas tank ran out of gas. He could really cook on the old wood-burning stove. Sometimes after a long day at work, he still would muster up the energy and strength to make it happen. We all awaited his delicious meals.

Tojo taught me most of the basic survival skills over several years, and he taught me about life as he and I knew it. Sometimes he'd drop me off at the nearest creek or pond to fish along the banks. When I wasn't in school, he would often allow me to go along with him to town or to his friends' homes.

I remember being with him when he plowed fields with the tractor. Sometimes we would get so dusty, and we would both have to wear scarves and sunglasses if we had any at the time. If we didn't, which was most of the time, then a cut-off piece of an old tee shirt had to suffice. Yes, these were the humblest times that I faced in life, but reflecting back on it now, it was all worth the journey.

Tojo taught me how to work on cars, build with wood, cut down trees, and plant a garden. My older siblings were too busy growing up and didn't spend much time during those early years with him. They were busy finding their way in life through trial and error. I was the next eldest at home and oftentimes found myself spending time with him as often as I could. I cherish the time spent with him. When he passed away, I was an adult living away from home. His death left me saddened and heartbroken, but I knew that I had to continue on. I just started reflecting on the joyous and grand times that we'd had together.

Be encouraged.

Deuteronomy 31:6: "Be strong and of good courage, do not fear nor be afraid of them; for the Lord your God, He is the One who goes with you. He will not leave you nor forsake you" (NKJV).

You are equipped by Father God for the long haul and are destined to achieve your goal as you stay focused. Just do not give up.

10

A Happy Father's Day That Never Was

My older siblings had their own father, rather a "dad." My own father was never present or engaged in any of his four children's lives either. At an early age I was aware that their dad would send my mother a fifteen-dollar money order periodically. Oh yes! This was one hundred percent more than what my dad "the man" had ever provided to my mother for my care.

When I was growing up, family members, friends, and even strangers used to call me Little Jack and Strom, I never knew all that they knew, but quickly learned that a community and neighbors would talk, and the word got around about who my mother's children belonged to. I grew up having to endure people calling me Little Jack before I even knew who Jack was. Other people already knew more about my father than I did. They also speculated on who my younger siblings belonged to as well.

A lot of people must have felt that it was their place to have and share their opinions about my mother's business. Both sides of my mother's family (aunts, first and second cousins, etc.), her in-laws, and even my schoolteachers all asked at one time or other about how many children there were in my family and who had fathered them. Sometimes they asked me, and at other times, they even were brave enough to ask my mother directly. Some of the comments directed at my mother were "Gee, are all those your children?" "How many children *do* you have?" "Don't your child, children look like this or that parent?" (Fill in the blanks!)

Because my mother's husband lived permanently in New York, his family members, such as a sister and some nieces (namely two particularly nosy ones) stated to others that I was not their cousin, but that my mother was their aunt; rather, she was their sister who, by the way is fair-complexioned and has green eyes unlike anyone else in the Seawright family. Some would tell my mother's husband that my mother was still having children despite not living with him anymore. Obviously, he had moved on too since he lived with another woman for the rest of his life in New York and had fathered other children as well. His family made it a mission to spy on and disparage my mother despite her husband's permanent absence from South Carolina from the late fifties onward. Why should he had been the only one to have moved on with life? I never saw him and my mother together again.

Several of our teachers asked us, "Do all of you have the same daddy?" Or they would say, "You look like __." I was always amazed at the audacity of all of these people to even question us about our personal family business. *Why* would they ask a child anything like that? It was utterly rude and disrespectful to say the least. But these questions did put me on a path of solving these uncertainties about my parentage. I had to take this mystery on.

At this juncture, I saw that other neighborhood parents had skeletons in their own closets. They didn't want their secrets to be divulged by their children or others. They probably had more skeletons in their closets than what the law would allow; for instance, having affairs with their pastors or fathering children all over the place with several women while married. This was and still is so taboo and unspoken about; at least it was not spoken about openly. Yet they would gossip amongst themselves about my mother. Even though they presented many questions to my mother, no one ever intervened or lent a hand to help support us. People would have everything to say about someone else's business, but they didn't show any compassion. Where were their hearts?

Today, there are millions of children, young and old, who are still trying daily to cope with being motherless and, especially, fatherless because of desertion by choice. The missing parent's family is also nowhere to be found, sometimes until their children have become successful in life and have become contributing citizens in society. *Now* they want to claim their children as their own. But where were they when the children needed them the most?

They had a break in life from hard work and dedication to having and doing more. In some cases, some deadbeat-come-lately "parent" and his family members are now proud of his successful children, and he wants to now act as an involved parent, knowing that he never contributed to his children's lives in any way up to that point. In my case, I wished my mother had filed for child support and had held that person accountable for what he caused as well as for what he didn't do for me. But my beautiful mother made many sacrifices while raising us to the best of her ability with God's help.

In order to survive all that came with my life, I learned, as I grew older, that there's a lot to life that I didn't know or understand because of my youth. By writing this book, I'm sharing my personal story and creating a living legacy for my children and grandchildren, with the support of my awesome spouse, Patrice.

OVERCOMING

Periodically, I walked to town to hang out in front of the club that was across the street from the town's Mayberry-like jailhouse, which was adjacent to my family church, Sardis Missionary Baptist Church. People there would point out the physical characteristics of my dad, Jack, and granddad, Yank Stroman, that they saw in me. I would see my granddad across the street at the gas station, pumping gasoline, but I'm now unable to recall him, like his son, ever acknowledging me.

They both would see me but never engage in a conversation with me. Neither of them ever acknowledged me as a son or grandson or even a little poor boy who yearned for the opportunity to know and grow up with his daddy and granddaddy. They never offered me a penny or bought me anything *ever*. Well, I *do* remember receiving a pair of jeans and a flannel shirt allegedly from Jack when I was eight years old. One of my mother's first cousins brought the clothes to me and said that my dad had bought them for me. Somehow, that just doesn't ring true. Why wouldn't he give them to me directly? Perhaps this cousin bought the clothes herself and just pretended that they came from him. That would be more logical to believe.

I saw my dad in town on numerous occasions. He would sit in his blue Ford pickup truck and just look at me but would never speak to me. Maybe he was afraid that I would ask him for something, but for something that he really owed me in every way. Instead, he decided to act as if I didn't exist. He persistently shunned, avoided, ignored, and rejected me. He dodged his responsibilities toward me for all the years of his natural life.

Maybe I was fearful to say anything to him, and he wouldn't initiate a conversation with me. But he seemed to never have a problem engaging with others. I didn't understand those moments either. My dad was a trustee in his home church for decades until his death in 2018. During his funeral, people spoke about his responsible nature toward the church. For example, several people spoke of how he had built an awning over the front doors to shelter people from the rain, and how he kept the church grounds clean and clear of debris. He was held in high regard as a trustee.

Not everyone is appointed as a trustee. People must believe that you can be trusted with great physical and financial responsibility for the care and upkeep of the church. Being a trustee in the church is a big deal. The pastoral staff and congregants trust a trustee to take care of the needs of the church and its members. Well, why didn't my father feel the need to trust himself with providing for all his children?

My dad had great jobs and lived with his wife and three other children in Columbia, South Carolina. He attended the area trade school in Denmark, South Carolina, and became a master builder, working mainly as a brick mason. Later, he landed permanent employment with the University of South Carolina, a position which he made a career, and he retired after many years. So, he had the assets and income to support me, but he refused to do so for reasons I wasn't clear on. Later, a sibling revealed to me that he would rent acres of land just to hunt on! I'm sure that was quite expensive. So, this man had all kinds of resources but didn't share with his children who weren't his wife's.

My dad fathered several other children before his marriage. I cannot honestly say if he did so during his marriage. But, at the very least, I don't think he ever stopped his philandering ways. Along with myself, two brothers, and two sisters (the older son had a twin sister who didn't survive) were born before his marriage. I just think it's highly unlikely that he wouldn't have had any other children besides us five that didn't belong to his wife. I've always heard that it's hard for a leopard to change its spots.

So I grew up not knowing what it was like to be in his presence and have a conversation about anything. I just felt that he never cared about or was interested in my well-being—physical, emotional, or financial. I also felt that he was coldhearted, uncaring, and selfish when it came to me. But I believe that he had no problem taking care of his wife and children while negating his total responsibility for me.

In my early years, my mother *never* spoke to me concerning anything about my dad and his side of the family. What's crazy about it all was that many people knew facts but never shared them with me. However, when my granddad died (I believe I was around fourteen or fifteen years old), my mother told me about it. She had purchased me a suit so that I could attend his funeral. Of course, no one from his family, not even my dad, told me about Yank's death or even offered to take me to his funeral. A friend of the family, B. K., picked me up from the old shack across the creek and dropped me off at Smyrna Baptist Church, which was Granddad's family church and where he was eulogized and laid to rest.

After the funeral, I had to catch a ride from the church to Granddaddy Yank and Grandmother Clyde's home because my mother had sent refreshments with me to give to the family, which I did. While I was at that house, my dad, his spouse, and their three children never acknowledged me at all. Even though they knew who I was, they never checked on me. O one of my half-siblings approached me and said, "You're not my brother, and you're not staying here tonight!" I don't recall which of the three said it to me, but he was a little younger that I. However, he couldn't have thought to make this comment on his own!

This is what's called learned behavior. Children learn behavior from the adults in their lives. I was overly surprised but took it in stride, as I kept pacing back and forth in the house. Over the span of around three to five hours, I continued to pace the floors throughout the house, but none of them—my dad, his spouse, my grandmother, or half-siblings—engaged me except to tell me who I wasn't and where I wasn't going to stay that night. No one was interested in making sure that I had anything to eat or a way back home. After that funeral, I don't recall ever seeing my half siblings again until our Grandmother Clyde's funeral in the nineties. There was no communication, no nothing. I've probably seen them two or three times within a forty-year span. Some royal treatment I received for just being a human being! That side of my biological family was so coldhearted, unaffectionate, and uncaring toward me. I thought that they would prefer that I would cease to exist or just go away quietly. They gave me that impression each time I saw them. I didn't understand why and have had to deal with this mystery for over fifty years.

While I was trying to figure out how I was going to get back home that night, I saw my dad sitting on the back porch. He refused to speak to me or have any contact with me. Now the time was getting late, and my dad's brother-in-law *finally* took me to town and dropped me off at the end of the long, lonely path to my house. I had to walk and sometimes run the rest of the way home alone in the pitch-black darkness of the night.

This was during the crazy times of the sixties. I experienced cars stopping and men getting out to chase me and try to do harm to me. So I routinely ran through the woods and sometimes hid in ditches until they gave up chasing me or just left altogether. Running or walking through the woods wasn't always fun. Sometimes, I got cut by thorns or even was stuck in the eyes by low hanging tree limbs. I would hear creepy sounds and voices. I sometimes felt that I was being "accompanied" by creeping humans as well. And I knew that my mother and siblings didn't have the slightest idea where I was.

I would pray to God to get me home safely. Most of the times, I wouldn't have any idea where I could exit from the woods or how close I would be to the house. I would sometimes come out far away from home because I had run in a circle. But when I did arrive home, thanks to God, my mother and siblings greeted me, and that gave me a good feeling about having arrived at a safe haven.

I must speak to this in hopes that this will encourage someone else who may have experienced the same disregard and disrespect. If you have, please, just stay encouraged and believe that God will handle all the negligence and maltreatment visited upon you. Karma has no respect of persons. What goes around sure enough does come back around. One reaps what one sows' All must stand before judgement and give an account to God of their lives and actions on Earth.

11

Chased by Tony the Bully

My siblings and I would regularly walk or run across the creeks and on into town. But on the way, sometimes I experienced drama and problems with some of the town bullies. One character was named Tony. He drove the extermination tractor as we called it in those days. He threatened to run over my siblings and me whenever he saw us walking to town together. We would take off into the woods to avoid him. Well, on one day, it seemed that ole Tony timed his approach exactly right and knew just about when we were heading to town.

When he could not successfully do us any harm, he sought then to harm our beloved dog, Brownie. As Brownie followed behind us and barked at the tractor while trying to fend off our tormentor, Tony lowered the arms of the insecticide sprayer and sprayed Brownie! Later, Brownie succumbed to the poison and died.

Brownie's death was so devastating to me and the whole family, for he was our beloved family pet, and it saddened us tremendously to watch him die. By the time we arrived up town, we encountered Tony giving us the "stare down" while telling us that he was going to "get" *us* some day as well. To say the least, we were frightened of Tony and of his darn tractor. While it was fun to him, it was not funny at all to us. Early on, we didn't pay a lot of attention to racism or prejudice. We had some great community neighbors throughout.

We attended a now desegregated school system, and my mother and grandmother, along with my siblings and me, would visit a host of Caucasian friends. Ms. N. loved for me to comb and brush her hair. Strangely, she cried frequently for whatever reason. I thought it was because she was "toasted" (in other words, drunk). I served as her hair "stylist" as she conversed with my mother and grandmother.

Man, I would dread having to be the only one that she would call upon to the unwelcomed duties of combing and brushing her hair. But of course, we were taught to honor and obey our elders and do what we were told, and we were not asked most times. If I had said no, my mother or grandmother would have disciplined me in one way or another.

Keep in mind that children were seldom allowed to be in the company of adults, but I was allowed to be present in their company because I was Ms. N.'s hair combing and brushing flunky. This was something that occurred often, unbelievably. To think about it today, it's very weird that I, of all people, was entrusted to comb this Caucasian lady's hair. Strange indeed.

Little did they know that I always wanted to be exempted from being in the company of adults during those times. My siblings would be outdoors playing with our white neighbors, having the grandest time of their lives. Once I had met Ms. N.'s standards (and my wrist and arms were tired and hurting), she would thank me and tell me that I could go outside and play with the other children. This usually happened right when it was too late and was getting too dark to play! Soon, it was time for all of us to be on our way back home through the fields and the manmade pathways.

These events would go on to shape my perception and opinions about race and bias in my life, and in my relationship with people of other races. As I have mentioned, we had decent neighbors for the most part, including some Caucasian families. I haven't allowed those two Caucasian people to "color" my judgment of people who didn't look like me. But these experiences helped to shape my character in that, as I would learn throughout my life, people are people, and they are the same everywhere, no matter their race or beliefs.

As a result of being intimidated and used as a flunky servant by some Caucasian people, I learned that it doesn't matter what color you are, but rather that we must always be respectful and mindful of how we treat others.

I don't judge people by their race, for I can attest to multiple accounts of being afforded opportunities or receiving help from people who didn't look like me. I caution everyone, young and old, to always consider how it would make you feel if someone didn't treat you kindly or consider you worthy as a human being based on your skin color. Give respect where and when it's due. Give Father God the opportunity to right those wrongs against you when some ignorant, hateful people don't appreciate your humanity and don't give you the chance to befriend them because of some hidden or blatant prejudice.

The righteous way is Jesus Christ.

John 14:6: "Jesus answered, 'I am the way and the truth and the Life. No one comes to the Father except through me.'"

Our Lord and Savior, Jesus Christ, is the only way. Trust Him always and you will have joy, peace, and rest in Him.

12

My Elementary Education Experience

L et's expound a little more on my school years.

We had to start preparing for another week of school. I loved school and had a burning desire to learn and be taught by some of the greatest schoolteachers. To this day, that burning desire has never left my consciousness. It's what saved me from a mundane life, and it made me feel and think that anything's possible with an education. I know that it's not on everyone's radar, but it's always been on mine because the possibilities have been endless for me.

And God made it possible for my mother to wake us up to get ready for school. I remember that year-round, we had to haul water and take our baths in the evenings, for waiting until the morning to take our baths would be too risky and would make us subject to catching colds.

Mother would have us go through the woods to buy kerosene or coal oil and single packs or books of matches from the stores uptown. The coal oil enabled us to start a fire and to have some for the kerosene lamps that we used for light. Mother never complained to us about our living conditions and the humbling experiences that we were facing year in and year out.

These sobering and trying times never gave us the leeway to think about what we didn't have or feel that we were experiencing an inadequate situation. Again, it's imperative to mention that my mother received only an occasional $15 in child support for my older siblings and *nothing* for the rest of the children, including myself.

Being in school physically gave me a different perspective on how unusual and barren my living conditions at home really were. Once I got to school and entered my classroom daily, I felt something totally different; for instance, I was able to use the school bathroom as authorized by my homeroom and only teacher. Something as simple as using indoor facilities meant a lot to me, and it made me realize that something so normal could mean so much to a little child like me.

My awesome first grade teacher, Mrs. W., was tall and beautiful. She had a big, bright, and beautiful smile, and she walked and spoke with elegance. She consistently displayed patience, professionalism, and a lot of love and concern for her whole class. She taught me how to read using the book series Dick and Jane. I still remember Dick, Jane, a dog named Spot, and a teddy bear named Puff. If I'm remembering right, Dick and Jane's mother had blonde hair.

For the most part, my classmates and I all stayed in one classroom, and all our subjects were covered by one teacher. Mrs. W. was an all-around educator. This is unheard of today. So without a doubt, things have really changed over the past decades.

When I didn't have the proper hair grooming on some school days, Mrs. W. would comb my hair with a pinecone, especially if she didn't have her hair comb or if I had too much hair to brush or comb with a regular comb. Mrs. W. and other teachers gave us one-on-one teaching. If we didn't learn our lessons or anything at all, then it was because we didn't try hard enough or want to learn. Every one of us sat upright at our desks, looking bright-eyed and bushy-tailed, motivated to learn every day.

Mrs. W. was a notable stickler for discipline and didn't tolerate any harsh or strange looks from her students. There was no talking back when we were being disciplined; today, we call it being "checked." When she had to, and one of us antagonized her, she would spank us on the buttocks or across her lap with a belt or ruler, and then we'd straightened right out once we finished crying or feeling embarrassed. I felt, afterwards, that we got just what we needed in the way of discipline.

She would call the attendance roll, and we would respond appropriately by answering her with "Here" or "Present, Mrs. W." Even though she would take attendance once a day, she always knew where each of us was at any given time. There was a student bathroom in the hallway for each of the four classrooms that were situated in each building. There were three buildings, a playground, and a baseball field on the entire school campus.

I thought that this was the largest school that had ever existed. Today, one would call this small-town thinking.

The first building accommodated the cafeteria and stage area, where we would eat, attend sock parties, and hold chapel devotions. Also in this first building were the administrative and principal's offices, the nurse's office, the janitorial storage closet, and other restrooms, primarily for the principal, faculty, and staff.

The other two buildings housed our classrooms and restrooms. Each accommodated eight teachers and their students. Back then, there weren't any paraprofessionals or assistant teachers in our schools. The eight teachers ran their own classrooms without assistance from additional staff. Today, there are assistants for every team of students. In my day, our teachers worked solo in all aspects of our school experience. So thinking back on this makes me really admire those educators and their dedication to us students when they had really only themselves to rely on in a group of many children.

I feel that this was very commendable. Now it's uncommon to have a "one-stop shop" in any classroom. Our teachers were the stars of the classroom, and everything centered on them. They made us feel that everything centered on us. Those teachers cared for their students in ways that parents would care about their children. I truly admire that about them, and I have even gone back home to my schools to present certain educators with tokens of my appreciation. They genuinely cared about us students, and we felt their love and concern for our well-being. My children's school experience has definitely not been the same as it was for me.

Today, many educators aren't concerned with the whole student. Today, the focus has shifted to how well or not so well students measure up to the national standard. My point in saying all of this is that educators are definitely different from the way they used to be in my day. This makes me sad and disappointed for my children. They're missing out on the way teachers actually took time out to get to know their students as people and were concerned about their progress in school. In my experience dealing with my children's teachers, I have found that most don't care if children pass or fail, or if they're even safe at home. I owe a debt of gratitude to my former teachers, from elementary to high school and beyond. My teachers' dedication to my education has left an indelible mark on every aspect of my life. Education represented freedom through thoughts and ideas of what is and what could be. That's the kind of freedom that no one can ever take away from us. And this quote is quite true and impressive: "A mind is a terrible thing to waste." This was part of a campaign slogan used by the United Negro College Fund in 1972 and to drive home the point of the necessity of education?

Come, all ye teachers, and help all children.

Deuteronomy 6:6–9:

> These commandments that I give you today are to be on your hearts. Impress them on your children. Talk about them when you sit at home and when you walk along the road, when you lie down and when you get up. Tie them as symbols on your hands and bind them on your foreheads. Write them on the doorframes of your houses and on your gates.

Proverbs 22:6: "Start children off on the way they should go, and even when they are old, they will not turn from it."

Be your child's first teacher. It's our responsibility as parents to nurture and train our children in the way they should go. It is not the responsibility of schools or the government; it is ours as parents, especially fathers who are worthy enough to be called father, like our Heavenly Father God.

Dads, spend time with your children, for it is not wasted time. You must engage your children in the kind of deep, heart-to-heart conversations that impart more than facts, but that teach wisdom as well.

13

As the School Days Turned

O ur teachers were human like anyone else. They gossiped and had lives in and outside the classrooms. They talked about each other, and sometimes they talked about us students. As I recall, there wasn't an intercom system in our schools. If a teacher or staff member needed to speak with or just relay a message to another person, they'd either have a student carry a sealed note during the school day, or they would just visit that classroom themselves, for there was nothing left to chance as far as allowing some curious students to open and read a personal note that was not addressed to them.

As for me, there were certain times when I would have my hair hygiene called into question, and my educators made sure to answer the call! Somehow, word got to my principal about my "hair situation," and he seemed to have the absolute worst timing when it came to remedying my dilemma. Whenever I was pulled away from class by the principal, I knew what was about to happen. *Why* did he have to think about cutting my hair right before lunchtime and recess? As a child, I was extremely sensitive about getting haircuts because of the scars I had incurred in an accident when I was around age three. I received permanent scarring as a result of falling out of a rocking chair into the fireplace. Although I was rescued from the fire before any other part of my body was consumed by fire, I nevertheless suffered from third-degree burns to my scalp.

Today, I'm very blessed to have lived to tell the story. I'm much more resilient these days as an adult and better equipped emotionally to handle criticism or ridicule. But imagine being six or seven and having other children laugh at you when you got a haircut that showcased something so devastating and frightening to have experienced as a child. Children can be very cruel; rarely are they understanding or compassionate. They, in fact, will mention the very things you wish to never discuss. My haircut days at school are some of the days I wish never happened, but these experiences helped shape who I am now.

The principal, Mr. C. B., would escort me to his office in building number one and cut my hair until I was bald—and I mean *bald*. I would cry each time he did this for several reasons. For example, I had tight curls that would get caught in the cross-blades. This really hurt and sometimes would even draw a little blood or leave yet another scar. My hair was quite thick, but Mr. C. B. seemed to not have very much mercy on my head when cutting my hair. There were no electrical shavers or trimmers, so he used either manual clippers or a straight-edged razor. And don't even mention the lack of shaving cream or something to help ease the effects of it all. Mr. C. B. got straight to business, and I had *no* say in how things were going to happen.

I was very embarrassed when he cut my hair down to the scalp because I have a deep gash and obvious scars on my head. The children would thump me on the head and call me "scalped up" or "burnt up head." So to say the least, I never looked forward to getting haircuts by Mr. C. B. Of course, he didn't have time to throw me a pity party. So, I often would have my personal moments and pity parties in the bathroom. Afterwards, I had to return to the classroom with the other children or report directly to the cafeteria. They were just waiting and anticipating the moment of my return so they could have their personal field day picking on me and calling me names due to my haircut and scarred head.

As a child, I didn't quite understand why I couldn't just have gotten a trim or a haircut that wouldn't emphasize my scars. Although the timing of it all was bad for me, I knew that my teacher and principal meant well. It helped me to have and maintain a good presentation. Even though these were some embarrassing times for me, I understand that it was done from a compassionate place, and I'm thankful for that.

But I digress. Back to learning how to read and write. By this time, I knew that I was left-handed. Others noticed it as well and felt that I was different and looked "funny" as they would say. It was awkward when I had to angle my papers in order to properly align my words when writing. At this initial juncture of learning, spelling was my main strength, and I always made straight As on spelling tests. This made me feel good, and it encouraged me to always do my best at whatever I was learning in and out the classroom. I also looked forward to lunch and recess so I could eat with my friends and play outside with them before having to return to the classroom.

Unlike the way it is today, as I recall, we didn't have many school or training holidays that required us to be out of school for a brief period. We didn't have early release days except maybe for the threat of inclement weather. On the rare occasion when we had snow, we had to make our snowmen quickly because the snow would often melt quite fast before we had the chance to really enjoy it. Our summers were long, and we didn't return to school until after Labor Day. Our summers lasted for a little over ninety days. I remembered playing outdoors for the entire summer. There were three more houses within sight of my house, but there weren't any young children to play with my siblings and me. We made up games as we went along. We played marbles and rolled old car tires and bicycle wheels. I made sand packers by piercing a small hole in the middle of a tin quart can, then punching a hole in the middle of both ends in order to run a wire clothes hanger through the middle of the can. Then I would fill it with mud or sand and wait for it to harden enough to prevent the sand or mud from running out of it before I had the opportunity to race or compete with it.

Then I would put the string on the outer part of the clothes hanger. We would pin clothes pegs to the wire so it would make a clapping sound as it touched the round portion of the can. We would also make it sound as if we were driving a real vehicle by making car or truck sounds. It was so much clean fun, and we would play until it was time to go in to eat or retire for the evening.

We couldn't afford many real toys, but I was able to buy some green plastic army soldiers to play with. We played jackstones with marbles as well. My siblings and I were not fortunate enough to have the luxury of owning bicycles at that time either.

14

The Ultimate Educational Challenges

A s I stayed out of school for the long summers, I wasn't motivated to go back to school in the fall. I was only six or seven years old and didn't realize the importance of getting the best education possible at that time. I realized that I had to increase my comprehension, retention, and application skills in order to be successful and to answer the call when life rang my bell to step up and become a contributing member of society. This was a must in order to obtain and apply a good education to my life. I must admit that this wasn't a priority to me initially.

There was no modern technology or great resources available in the 1960s and '70s. I didn't have access to a public library; the closest one was about eight miles away. I was a fast-paced walker but didn't always have the desire or time to walk that far to do any kind of research about anything.

So I would use the school library to read various books. The librarians were always available and extremely helpful to me. They pointed me in the right direction to find books in which I showed a great interest. The school library was the coolest and quietest place I had ever known. There wasn't any tolerance for loud noises or talking in the library, so you had to use your "indoor voice" at all times.

15

Moving On to the Second Grade

Cousin F. R. H. was my second-grade teacher, and she was so awesome in ensuring that we got the best education possible. Being in the second grade didn't present many differences or changes. Life was happening at a slow pace, so I thought. I was continuing to learn and grow into what is my life, with its expectations, struggles, and all that it had to offer. I had great teachers. They were very loving, approachable, and helpful. And they had a lot of compassion for us as students.

As school ended for the day, life held its own ongoing struggles at home. I would either go back to my home through the woods or go to my great-grandmother's home until my mother got off work and came to pick us up. Once I got home, I had to pitch in to assist my mother by gathering wood and water for the house and preparing for another day of school. Yes, this was a typical day in my life, living in the woods off that old dirt road.

I can do this!

Proverbs 3:5–6 "Trust in the Lord with all your heart; do not depend on your own understanding Seek His will in all you do, and He will show you which path to take."

Your Christian journey will not be easy, but God will give you strength to press on daily and overcome any situation. Even at a young age, you sometimes must apply yourself to be all that you can be, for it's all a part of your journey.

16

A Typical Day at Home and School—Enjoying the Third Grade and Life

A lthough I was young and having a lot of fun, it was also time to learn more. I gathered myself together and began learning what it was like to be a third grader and all that I needed to do in order to progress as I went through school. I still had to get up early in the morning to prepare for school, especially as I had to take that long walk through the woods if I missed the school bus. Sometimes I was afraid to trek through the woods alone. Sometimes it was cold and wet on my route to school, but this was all I knew and had to contend with.

Of course, I was okay once I arrived at school. I felt better and safer being around other children throughout the day. The security I felt when I was around others was important to me. Life was extremely hard on me and very challenging. Even though I didn't know a lot about life, I sensed that some things just didn't add up. I began to learn—and learn quickly—but I felt that something was missing from my life. I realized that I had no male role model in my life, specifically, my biological father. Although I didn't know who he was early on, I continued to go forward and do the best that I could, knowing that at least my mother loved me. I was never fully acknowledged by my dad throughout my entire life. This is so sad to say the least, but it never changed much, not even up to the day he died. Despite his lack of acknowledgment and support, I never disrespected or denied him as my biological father.

I knew how I felt inside, day in and day out, year in and year out, about not having my dad even celebrate with or wish me a happy birthday—*ever*! I never received child support, and I refused to display this type of behavior to my awesome, beautiful children, who are now mostly adults.

I guess, to finally provide *something* in way of support, he did provide the jeans and shirt. This was what I always remember ever receiving from my dad. For years, I really wanted to give that two-piece set back to him, so I would've been able to say that he'd never given me anything. He didn't give me the gift of his sincere presence in my life. This was traumatizing, disappointing, and very hurtful to say the least. It was a pivotal moment in my life when I realized that my dad wasn't one of my teachers. Thank God that He provided others.

OVERCOMING

Mrs. G. R. and Mrs. B. F. were both great teachers who ensured that we were disciplined and focused and that we understood the lessons they planned. They taught us what was expected of my classmates and myself. There was a lot of one-on-one time with my teachers until I had no other choice than to learn on my own. I had to stay focused as best as I could. At that time, there wasn't a lot of time for playing around in the classroom. Even though I liked learning, I also looked forward to resting periods.

We had recess and lunch. After that, it was back to the drawing board. We had a gigantic green board that was called the blackboard. My teachers used chalk to write with, spelling out words from the lessons of the day. I too had the opportunity to approach the green board and write something on it in front of my classmates. This was quite scary, but I was up for the task.

17

The Fourth Grade

My fourth-grade teachers were Mrs. C. and Mr. F. B. They were super awesome, always caring about my education and my overall welfare. Mr. F. B. was an amazing artist. He taught me how to draw and sketch. It became evident that he saw something in me than I didn't see in myself at that young age. He had so much patience, and he ensured that I understood the many instructions that he gave me. To me, it was all about learning and surviving from day to day.

These two teachers were preparing the other kids and myself for middle school. That school was A. L. Corbett Middle School, which was in another city called Wagener, eight miles away from the first and only school up to that point that I had ever known. So, I had to adjust to catching the school bus early enough to ride to A. L. Corbett. This was all foreign to me, and my narrow window of experience brought about many more challenges and experiences for me, to say the least. I learned many lessons about discipline. When I caused infractions, I received many whippings. I didn't just receive a light time out, or even verbal warnings; instead, I received whippings with either a ruler, a thick black belt, or a paddle with holes in it, which was designed to suck flesh through its holes.

I don't remember the teachers or the principal ever drawing blood when using these instruments. Sometimes a hard right- or left-handed slap on the face would suffice. Okay, you would call that child abuse today, but this was considered only minor discipline back in the day. Oh no, I couldn't mention any of this to my mother. If I did, I would've received even *more* chastisement and would've had a hard time resting in bed at night. So, I just took the whippings and kept on moving. But it's my fear today that this type of punishment would really cause traumatic experiences for practically all children. I wouldn't recommend this type of strict or extreme punishment today.

18

The Fifth Grade

I recall an incident that caused me to face a whipping. I picked on my classmate who was nicknamed Blue Jaybird Head. As punishment, I got a whipping across my buttocks while straddling the principal's "electric chair." Principal C. B. gave me the option to "choose" whichever "tool" he would use on me. He used the paddle with the multiple holes on my rear end. So, I got my punishment and went on with the rest of my day. I exited the school for the day, got on the bus, and headed home. When I got home, there was work to be done.

Even though the time we got out of school didn't vary that much, I still had chores to manage before it became too dark to see. I never had time to complain, pout, or cry about our living conditions. I just never really understood it myself. My awesome mother stayed on the grind trying to provide for the eight of us. She never complained to us about anything when it came to making provisions. But I believe that she would often have a long conversation with my Almighty Father God about her concerns relating to her family or life and what it offered her.

She didn't have time to make PTA meetings or assist us with

our homework. I don't recall ever bothering or asking my mother for any assistance. I knew I had to do my best in figuring out my lessons, even though the teachers tried to make sure we were well equipped. I loved learning and had to remember what I was being taught in order to test well.

My teachers took the time out to answer any questions that we had, so I was well informed about my lessons before I left school at the end of the day. I've noticed how the times in educational systems have drastically changed today. There are zero comparisons today to the times I came through school. Educators are simply different today. I'm grateful that I was taught by teachers who treated us as if we were their own.

The Sixth Grade

My sixth-grade year was more of the same—very like the years before. School continued to be a place where I flourished and yearned for more out of life. My family and I were still picking cotton in the landlord's cotton fields. We finally received our first black-and-white television, courtesy of my older half-sibling's grandmother who had a TV on layaway at a local store. When she passed away, someone paid for the TV. A family friend delivered it to our home while we were working in the fields. By this time, we had some consistent form of electricity. Our home life was still a struggle, but we had each other to lean on.

Stay focused, disciplined, and grounded in your journey.

John 9:4: "We must carry out the works of Him who sent me as long as it is day; night is coming, when no one can work."

OVERCOMING

Psalm 37:4: "Always delight yourself in the Lord and He will give you the desires of your heart."

We are to stay focused on the Lord, working hard and steadily. Weeping may endure for a night, but joy comes in the morning.

20

Two Staples of My Life:
Cotton and Church

P icking cotton. It was our way to make a living at the time. It was extremely hard, grueling work to say the least. Sometimes we would work the cotton fields until noon on Saturday and take off all day on Sunday, sometimes to attend church. My mother and grandmother loved the good Lord and tried their best to please Him by attending annual revivals and some Sunday services.

Usually, we had services only on second and fourth Sundays. During that time, not too many African American church doors were open on all four Sundays of the month. I'm not sure if it was a budget issue or if it was just some tradition for many of our churches. Maybe it was a combination of both. We would walk or catch a ride to our family church in Salley. I had liked going to Sardis Missionary Baptist Church, and years later, I worked there as a custodian. Often, when I was cleaning the church, I found myself mimicking the preacher by standing behind the pulpit and acting like I was preaching. During one particular year of the revival, I was nearly a pre-teen and was told by my mother and grandmother to get ready for a water baptism in order to join the church on that Friday, the final day of revival.

My older siblings had to prepare as well. We all arrived at the church a bit earlier than usual for this occasion. The baptismal pool was located outside the church, and there were walls around it. The pastor never offered me the plan of salvation; instead, he just baptized me in that pool. I felt no change of heart or mind during the process; I just concentrated on being almost drowned and how soaking wet it left me.

Afterward, we were directed to sit in the chairs positioned in front of the pulpit while we became a part of the physical church and were accepted as part of the church family itself. People came around to shake our hands in a show of welcoming us to the church family fold. While baptism for my siblings was traditionally acceptable, I didn't receive the Christian plan of salvation for my eternal soul. I was baptized as a dry sinner and came up from the water a wet sinner. I felt that there was no real change of heart in me. I didn't learn the importance behind salvation and baptism until much later in life through my religious studies and training. It has become my life-long mission to share their significance and application to our spiritual lives.

At the time, I wasn't tracking just how important the church and religion would be in my life journey. My spirituality is at the very essence of my being, and through the love and grace of Father God, I can live freely and to help others reach that level of freedom in Jesus. Life comes with its struggles, but I found out that, if you have the good Lord in your life, then nothing is impossible. Faith makes things possible. We endured a lot of struggles as we grew up, but we could always cling to the hope that things could and would get better.

Although I was "born again" in the Lord, I *still* had some old habits that died hard. Sometimes when people don't have things they need or want, they may resort to taking them. Like any other children, my siblings and I liked snacks, but most of the time, we didn't have the money to pay for them. I was the youngest of the group, so my older siblings made me the fall guy. We developed sticky fingers while shopping in one of our local mom-and-pop stores; one particular one was owned by the local Kennedy family.

One day, it was my turn to carry out the snacks to which we had helped ourselves. Standing at less than five feet tall, I looked funny with the sudden weight gain around my waist area. Mr. K. told me that I looked pregnant as I was leaving his store. Of course, I denied being pregnant, but he was insistent that I must've been because, when he squeezed my stomach, he felt something extra going on there. Of course, I denied that I knew anything about what he meant as I tried to make my way to the door— never mind that my brothers had left me alone in the store to fend for myself. Their only concern was when I would exit with their snacks. Well, Mr. K. and I continued with our little exchange about my sudden weight gain. He questioned me, and I stuck with my denials.

Seeing that I was sticking to my story, he finally lifted my shirt, and all the chips and other snacks fell to the floor. Of course, like a child who's been caught red-handed would do, I denied knowing how the snacks came into my possession. Being amused by this but wanting to make a point, he showed me to the door and pointed out to me and my siblings the town of Salley's little jailhouse that sat cattycorner to the store. He told us that we would wind up in there if we continued to steal from his store. That scared me straight because although I'd never been to jail before, it didn't seem like a nice place to be. I was scared just thinking about how bad it would be for a little kid like me. Word got around that the police chief was genuinely nice, but he was also serious about stopping crime in his town. That "scared straight" moment changed me for the better, and it caused me to think better the next time I allow others to influence me to do bad things.

21

The Seventh Grade— Junior High School

E ducation continued to be especially important and integral to my life. I wanted to learn how I could use it to contribute back to society. Again, I had very caring teachers. I enjoyed learning and realized that I had reached a higher level of understanding. I felt something different that I enjoyed, but I wasn't sure where I was heading in life. I became more curious and began to ask my teachers many more questions.

They later shared with me that I was going somewhere in life and that I was going to be someone special in this world. Initially I smiled, but I had many more uncertainties and unclear understandings after I heard this from them. The time had come for me to move on to the seventh grade. Two of my most influential teachers were Ms. R., the science teacher, and Mr. S., the agriculture teacher. Ms. R. taught me the meaning of the word *hypothesis*, which means an educated guess. I thought this word sounded big and important, and to this day, I have never forgotten it. Every time I think of this word, I think of Ms. R. She was the most awesome science teacher. Then there was Mr. S., who taught me all about farming, feed, cattle, cotton gins and combines, as well as planting. I fondly remember that he was knowledgeable, wise, and experienced. He always showed a lot of patience and professionalism as a teacher.

Another teacher taught me all the ins and outs of home economics—learning how to maintain a home in its entirety and how to prepare healthy but filling home-cooked meals for the family. I had a blast while learning more about life and its possibilities.

These educators wanted me to become well rounded in the world and society. They really took the time to show how much they cared. I knew they desired that I get a proper education.

I was learning and growing so much that, when we went out for recess or had a break from school, I was so excited when the breaks were over so I could return to the classroom where I was being taught by the best educators in the world. I'm sorry that I missed more opportunities than I made to take the time in my adult years to return home and thank my educators for all their dedication and time. So please don't neglect to take time out to return to your roots to thank, show love to, and hug your educators for what they have sown into your lives.

Over the past recent years, I was fortunate and mindful enough to do so. But I still feel bad that I lost total contact with most of them. By this time, some have passed on to a restful and peaceful place that they so deserved for their many tireless sacrifices.

22

Eighth Grade

Oh wow, finally the last year of junior high school! There were even more exciting but numerous uncertainties about what was ahead in life's plan for me. Yes, I was a "senior" junior high school student, and now officially a teenager. Still, there were not many major differences in my life now. But there were more expectations that I would do the right thing and continue my education in order to become all that I could be. The older I became, the more responsibilities I was required to assume.

During summer breaks, I would get a job working in the fields, harvesting watermelons and other kinds of vegetables and fruits for the white farmers. I would either make four to six dollars for one day's work or for the job itself, whichever the owner decided upon. Of course, it would be to his advantage, not mine. Either way, it was little pay for working in those hot, sweltering fields. Most times, I would work without eating breakfast and sometimes lunch too, and I would often get sick because I hadn't eaten any decent food.

No matter how much money I made, I would always give my mother at least half of what I had earned. She was very humble and thankful for what I shared with her. She never asked me for any of my earnings, but through my conscience and through Father God, I knew the right and moral thing to do was to share and give back to the one and only person who had taken care of me and raised me the best she could. This was only the beginning of so many blessings that Father God already had in store for me.

I spent part of the summer attending football, basketball, baseball, and track and field practices for the teams at the high school I would be attending. I had to either catch a ride or walk eight miles one way just to get to practice, but I was determined to be a part of those teams. I was a good enough player to make it onto the high school varsity football team while I was still attending junior high school. I felt that this was a huge accomplishment. I started gaining more and more confidence in whatever I pursued. After practice, I would have to flag someone down for a ride or just start walking the eight miles back home. Hey, I just had to do what I had to do (loved doing). I didn't totally realize what exactly this would lead to and how it would affect my future.

That summer, I also worked for the summer program of the Aiken County Community Commission Development Services. That opportunity and experience stayed with me for various reasons, but I remember it so well and often for several specific reasons. I was thirteen years old and would turn fourteen later that year. I had a great elderly role model, Mrs. M. D., who favored me and wanted me to have the opportunity to work a public job.

She was the director of that summer program. The pay afforded me the opportunity to make more money and buy my own supplies and clothing for the upcoming school year. She took me to town on paydays to cash my check and make purchases. One payday, Mrs. M. D. took me to a store in Wagener so that

I could finally make the last payment on and pick up the bike I had on layaway. I was so happy to have that brand-new yellow, twelve-speed bicycle. I asked Mrs. M. D. if I could ride it back home to Salley. Of course, her response was "Yes, sweetheart." She even took the time to follow me home to ensure that I made it there safely.

Oddly enough, she was also president of my local Boy Scout chapter. She and I got along so well that I wanted to be around her every chance I had. Mrs. M. D. was the only person I knew who could drink a bottle of Coke and not make one sound! She was so, so loving, supportive, and caring. Honestly, I just did not think that I deserved all the attention she gave me. She also started a baseball team and made me the pitcher.

She hauled our team around in her nice two-door Ford Gran Torino sports coupe, taking us to other towns for our games. She never asked for or expected any pay or gas money from us or our families. This generosity is almost unheard of today. I consider Mrs. M. D. as my guardian angel from heaven. Today, I would give a lot just to see her again and to let her know just how much I loved her for all that she had been to me. She was so impactful in my early stages of growth and development. Mrs. M. D. was such a godsend, and I never took her support for granted.

Hard work pays off.

1 Timothy 2:1–2: "I urge, then, first, that petitions, prayers, intercession and thanksgiving be made for all people for kings and all those in authority, that we may live peaceful and quiet

lives in all Godliness and Holiness. This is good and pleases God our Savior."

2 Thessalonians 2:16: "May our Lord Jesus Christ himself and God our Father, who loved us and by his grace gave us eternal encouragement and good hope, encourage your hearts and strengthen you in every good deed and word."

Having to do hard, labor-intensive work always builds character, strength, resiliency, and a stronger, more positive mindset and outlook on life. Only God can give you the motivation, spiritual insight, and ability to acknowledge, worship, and serve Him throughout your life, which in turn, makes you a better version of yourself and prepares you for what He has in store for you.

23

*Back to the Fields and
on to the Ninth Grade*

S oon the summer and work season for me was over and it was
time to return to school. I was ready and prepared in more
ways than one. At this time, I began to work less in the fields. One
certain crop owner was so racist that he would always make us take
off our shoes to work in his fields. Even at a young age, I knew that
something wasn't right about our working barefoot. But I noticed
that he would never take off his shoes. This was no laugh-out-loud
moment for me. It was about humiliation and maltreatment that
was unnecessary and unbecoming. I later realized that the racist

owner didn't want us to squash his precious crops. Imagine that he cared more about his crops than he did about us workers. But because we needed the money, my family and I did what we had to, even if it meant working in the fields barefoot. Now on to the ninth grade.

Yeah, yeah, yeah, I finally made it to the big leagues—to Wagener-Salley High School. This experience was like a new start because I had to meet and get to know my new educators, coaches, and principal. This was a true transitional moment for me, and I had to learn how to adjust to the conditions that existed. I felt that the process was a meaningful change of growth and realization.

I started counting the years that I had left before graduating from high school. My three older siblings were still attending high school as well. I would often see them throughout the day. Being present at the same high school as my siblings brought comfort and encouragement to me. I knew they were leading the way by setting an example for me to emulate in school.

Even though I had to learn on my own and get my education for myself, the teachers were there for my questions and concerns. I really loved attending school and didn't want to miss one day away from school. I had a true sense of belonging and felt that I was in the right place. But not knowing what was ahead of me, I just took life day by day.

Before I started attending high school, I had already joined several sports teams. The coaches quickly became my mentors and trainers for the next four years. They taught me a good way of life and instilled hard work and good morals in me. They had such wisdom and wise sayings and teachings that made life a little better for me. Unbeknownst to them, they really affected my life. They set me on a course of hope, reality, love, faith, and confidence that has stayed with me until this day.

My regret is that I left home a few years after graduating from high school and didn't return for many, many years. I really wanted to go back home and thank my coaches for the lasting impact they had on my life. Since I didn't have my dad in my life, these men took it upon themselves to instill in me what I know now should've come from my own father. I'm grateful to them for taking me under their wings and teaching me about sports, and more importantly, about life.

After sports practice, I would take a shower at the school. This would save me from having to use the foot tub to bathe in once I got home. Afterward, I had to find a ride home or just start walking the eight miles. If I had to walk home, then, yes, I had to wash up again before lying down for the night. But there was no comparison to taking a nice hot shower, for which I was thankful. Afterwards, I would sometimes stop in the neighborhood and catch up with some of my friends for a while before journeying on home, sometimes having to walk through the woods.

My mother would always rejoice with her beautiful smile upon my arrival home. Even though she didn't hold long, drawn-out conversations with me, I still knew and felt her love and support for me.

I had a great ninth-grade school term and I looked forward to what great things tenth grade could possibly hold. I hoped it would be a repeat of my freshman year, but I desired to soar to an even higher level in life and school. I had a true sense of belonging as well as confidence and hope. It seemed that things were beginning to look up and were favorable for me. Bye-bye, ninth grade. Are you ready for me, tenth grade?

Before I could start my tenth-grade year, there was the matter of attending my paternal grandfather's funeral. No need to rehash it though. I attended the funeral only out of obedience to and respect for my mother. To best sum it up, no one in that family ever acknowledged me as one of their own, and I'm unwilling to make up some nice fantasy about that whole side of my "family."

If it had been up to me, I really don't believe I would have even bothered attending Yank's funeral. To what avail? It only contributed to what I was feeling all along. That man, just like his son, my dad, never acknowledged me or considered me to be part his family. I wasn't cared for or cared about. *None* of them ever cared about my well-being. Although I truly existed, they all acted as if I didn't. It took me a long time to get over those feelings of resentment, lack of acknowledgment, and abandonment. Again, I had no idea why I was treated this way each time I saw them. It took me years to realize that there was nothing at all wrong with me, but everything was off kilter and wrong with them.

I learned this only with Father God's help, love, and grace. But as I know now, one reaps what one sows. Karma is real and has no respect of person. What goes around comes back round. We all reap what we sow, good or bad. If your number hasn't come up yet, just keep living, and it will. No millionaire or billionaire can buy or add one day to his or her life.

<hr />

Listen to your God-sent mentors who care about you.

Ephesians 4:11–12: "And he gave some, apostles; and some, prophets; and some, evangelists; and some, pastors and teachers; For the perfecting of the saints, for the work of the ministry, for the edifying of the body of Christ."

Romans 3:24: "Yet God in His grace, freely makes us right in His sight. He did this through Christ Jesus when he freed us from the penalty for our sins."

Stay encouraged while listening to those who care about you enough to love, mentor, and teach you the right way to go, for it will take you an exceptionally long way in life.

24

The Tenth Grade

Renee Salley
Annette Scott
Larry Seawright

In my tenth-grade year, I worked at the Wagener Manufacturing Plant, HNF, a shirt company, at the end of each school day. I would report to work before and after sports practice. I worked there off and on for several seasons before I graduated from high school.

I also found a job through Aiken County working in Salley as a groundskeeper. I was mainly responsible for landscaping and the overall upkeep of the entire little town of Salley. I worked three days a week. I also kept the city hall building clean. When I was initially hired for the job, for some reason, I thought that I was hired to work in the grocery store but realized that the store position had already been filled. I had really wanted that grocery store job but had to soon get over that wishful thinking.

As I worked on in a better job and got paid accordingly, I was able to share even more with my awesome mother to help her with the bills and other responsibilities.

25

The Eleventh Grade

During my eleventh-grade year, I attended both Wagener-Salley High School and Crescent City High School/ Trade School. Wagener-Salley High was getting full, so all of us students were given the option to attend both schools for the remainder of our junior and senior years. Most of us ended up taking classes at both schools. This option afforded me many great advantages.

One main advantage was that I was closer to home in Salley, which was just across the creeks. Also, my former elementary school teacher, Mrs. A. W., taught me math at the high school. I learned trigonometry and calculus in her classes. Several other teachers taught me a lot, and I took full advantage of the trades offered at Crescent City. Man, did I have fun learning! Every year, I felt, afforded me the opportunity to take on new trades that I might be able to use later in life.

My older brothers attended these schools as well, and they caught on quickly to learning the various trades. But soon, all three of them somehow grew weary of school and decided to quit as sophomores and juniors. One was very gifted in auto mechanics and performed many jobs in that arena and maintained the shop cars. To this day, he still does that kind of work successfully.

26

Life-Changing Experiences

During my eleventh-grade year, upon my mother's insistence, I went to live with some of her relatives to help them out. I took up residence with my great-uncle, "Booster"; my great-grandmother, O. G. ("Granny"); and later on, my great-aunt, Sarah. My mother saw that Uncle Booster was taking care of his mother, Granny, alone. Because some of his siblings were away from home or were just preoccupied with their own families and lives, I was tasked with helping them out around the house. Granny was getting older and was no longer able to take care of herself. Uncle Booster had never married, and so he took it upon himself to care of his mother. I moved in with them to help with chores. I also drove a school bus and played sports year-round. Wow, as if I wasn't busy enough! But I took everything in stride and kept moving.

There was no such thing as disobeying my mother. But you would've thought that another of Granny's children or grandchildren would've stepped up to the plate and helped us to care for her daily. To this day, I've often wondered why I was chosen out of all my mother's older children to act as caretaker to my great-grandmother along with my great-uncle. But, if I had to guess, my mother must've felt that I was very responsible and caring. She knew that I was obedient to and respectful of my elders, as she had taught me to be. I think it all taught me to care about others who couldn't take care of themselves as they normally would have, and to realize that family is the most important asset you have in times like those. Although I was still very young, I was set on a course that proved to shape my outlook on life, health, and the treatment of others who are left in your charge. Although I wasn't looking for anything, I was blessed by the good Lord to have gone through that experience. It taught me about compassion and understanding. I'm the better for it.

Live with compassion, obedience, and service to others.

Ephesians 4:32: "Be kind and compassionate to one another, forgiving each other, just as in Christ forgave you."

Ephesians 6:1: "Children, obey your parents in the Lord, for this is right."

Proverbs 19:17: "Whoever is kind to the poor lends to the Lord, and He will reward them for what they have done."

27

My Senior Year—A Transitional Period

One Step From Heaven . . .

First Row: W. Horsey, K. Felder, J. Worrell, M. Ginyard, M. Ginyard, L. Seawright
Second Row: S. Thomas, J. Schofield, N. Sampson, D. Frazier, C. Brown

Yes, my final year in high school had come. It was bittersweet to say the least. I had a variety of positive and negative thoughts about what would happen next and what I was really going to do after graduation. I knew that I would miss playing sports year-round. Playing football, basketball, baseball, and running track and field were all fun to me. The coaches all had a major influence on my life in those years of high school. They were not only my coaches, but they were also father figures and mentors to me.

I was committed to playing sports, and so I made the sacrifice to make sure that I could participate no matter what. Sports provided an outlet and taught me about discipline and commitment. Since transportation was still a hit-and-miss issue for me, I'd grown to like walking home alone. I picked treats along the way home including black and red berries, cherries, cinnamons from a cinnamon tree, pears, and pecans. By the time I arrived home, I was pretty full of all my snacks. Most times, but not always, I arrived home before nightfall. I'd still arrive just in time to complete my chores, like hauling water and wood and raking the yard in preparation for another day.

I would also miss working part time at the Wagener Manufacturing Plant before heading off to football practice. I also worked at the Graniteville Cotton Mill during my senior year of high school. The city of Graniteville is located about thirty miles away from home. But I made the sacrifice to travel that far to work. Some of my high school peers and I drove to work to Graniteville and worked from four in the afternoon to midnight during the week.

I worked as a doffer – this is someone who removes ("doffs") bobbins, pirns or spindles holding spun fiber such as cotton or wool from a spinning frame!, removing full bobbins of spun cotton and replacing them with empty ones. This resulted in cuts to my hands and fingers. While on probation, I often worked without getting or having the opportunity to take a break, but I would take this in stride and strive to do my best anyway that I could. I didn't complain. There was no time for that. Work and school were a part of my weekly routine. But now that I was going to be graduating from high school, I had to figure out what was next for me.

The bittersweet moments of transition and of doubts about what was ahead caused me to keep the faith and never cease to pray for a better tomorrow. We sometimes understand what is behind us, but we have faith and hope for progression to push forward, as life can be a total mystery. Sometimes change and challenges are good for growth and maturity, for you cannot buy experience.

<hr />

Always maintain the I-can attitude, and wait on the Lord.

Philippians 4:6–7, 13, 19

> Do not be anxious about anything, but in every situation, by prayer and petition, with thanksgiving, present your requests to God. And the peace of God, which transcends all understanding, will guard your hearts and your minds in Christ Jesus.

> I can do all things through Christ who strengthens me.

> For my God shall supply all my needs according to his riches in glory by Christ Jesus.

28

The Blue Plant and College

Eventually, I resigned from Graniteville Cotton Mill and started working at the shirt factory in Wagener. Soon, I resigned from there and went on to work at the (shirt factory) Blue Plant in Salley, which was closer to home. I was hired by a friend of my biological father. She favored me for the job because of her association with him. Anyway, I was happy to get the job.

While working there, I met a great woman who saw my potential, or at least something in me that I didn't see in myself. She told me that I was too young to spend any more time in that factory. She said that I needed to get out of the factory and consider college, which at that point, had never been mentioned to me before. Plus, I had no leads on how to pursue even looking into going to college. Therefore, there wasn't any encouragement, especially from family, to attend college.

But I kept this in the back of my mind and started contemplating, or at least considering, attending college. I don't recall being encouraged to attend college, not even by my educators, neighbors, or so-called friends. For the most part, when my contemporaries finished high school, they went to work in the local factories or got a job elsewhere. Some would go into the military.

Another great mentor who also knew my dad approached me during a church anniversary service about college too. She initially encouraged me to consider attending Denmark Technical College, and she told me she would assist me in getting funding for college. Financial help was based on family income, and due to my mother's low income from picking cotton, I was sure to qualify for grants that would afford me the opportunity to attend school.

I could never forget or neglect to appreciate those great and inspiring people who cared enough about me and believed in me. They inspired me to know my worth after my years of searching for what was or could be my purpose and reason for living.

Encourage the potentials in others.

Proverbs 4:18: "The path of the righteous is like the morning sun, shining ever brighter till the full light of day.

Isaiah 60:1: "Arise, shine, for your light has come, and the Glory of the Lord rises upon you.

Let your acts of encouragement toward others become a vital part of your everyday life. You never know what your positive words can do for another person. Don't ever think that you can't be a light in someone's dreary day.

29

The Job/Career Challenge and College

I left the factory in Salley in search of a better way of life. Then I linked up with one of my siblings and started driving a medical transportation van for the Aiken County Community Action Commission (ACCAC). Ms. B. P. was the amazing director at the ACCAC. She was so inspiring to me every time I heard her speak. She was a committed supporter of Dr. Martin Luther King Jr. and his fighting cause for civil rights for all.

Getting into college and staying on campus in the dorms was an experience like no other. Up to that point, and aside from staying temporarily with other family members to help care for my loved ones, I had never lived away from home. College was a time for me to spread my wings and soar. I wanted to take full advantage of the college experience. I knew it would take me to greater heights and afford me the future I had always believed existed.

I finally left home for college and didn't look back in wonder at what I was leaving behind; neither did I know what was before me. But I was ready and up for the challenge. This move was the best thing that had ever happened to me. But I needed a reliable job to go along with the support that I was receiving through grants. Then I began a plan to move forward and to get a real career going and to be successful in my decision-making process. I began considering joining the US Army. I liked college, but I realized that I had to start looking elsewhere in order to get to the places I wanted to be.

Over the years, all my siblings, especially the three oldest living ones, had the same equal opportunity that I had to pursue the greatness of all that life had to offer, and they chose to live in our hometown, get jobs, work hard, and raise their families. It's all about choice. Whatever choices they made, they were willing to live with I chose to leave home and believe that I could and would do better than what was available to me at that point in time.

So, of us four older living children, I was the first to finish high school, the only one who ever attended and finished college, the only one who joined the military and retired after serving over thirty-eight years for this great country. Plus, I was the only one who ever worked for the US government aside from serving in the military. I was the only one who traveled abroad to numerous countries and visited forty of our fifty United States!

Now reflecting over my life, I know I would do it all again the same way if the opportunity presented itself. Don't hate the player; you can hate the game. I just felt that there was more to life and hope for a brighter future than what was before me. I set out to pursue it and discovered that life had a world of experiences to offer. I just had to get out of my comfort zone and go for it with drive and focus. By doing so, I surely expanded my horizons. My mother would often remind me of how proud she was of me, and that was all that ever mattered to me. I wanted to make her proud of me and show others around us that it could be done. Perseverance and hard work count and go a long way.

Where I grew up, it seemed abnormal for one to really soar high and become successful. Many people were stuck in their own ways and were not happy to see others rise to another level. I call it small-town thinking. If it were the other way around, I would congratulate them and be so happy for anyone to become successful.

So I know that I am blessed by God, who reminds me that I am somebody also. The one who was underestimated and not thought to be anything became somebody. I'm not sorry for anyone's disappointment of what Father has instilled in me, but I am more sorrowful for all my haters and naysayers.

Keep going and love them with God's agape love anyway!

Matthew 5:44: "But I tell you, love your enemies and pray for those who persecute you."

John 15:20: "Remember what I told you: a servant is not greater than his master. If he persecuted me, they would persecute you also. If they obeyed my teaching, they would obey yours also."

God's will is for us to love each other as we love ourselves. Despite how you're treated, still obey those who have authority over you. Don't fret—Father God won't allow them to destroy you. Keep doing the right thing, and you'll be blessed for it.

30

Suicidal Thoughts and Contemplation

Due to the ongoing financial struggles experienced by my family and me, as I would walk to and from town, crossing the two bridges, I often contemplated committing suicide in order to alleviate some of the burden from my mother. I wanted my deficient way of life to be over! Life just seemed too tough to live. I didn't think to ask my mother if she could afford life insurance or even if she had a policy on us children. I could've been a total loss, but there would've been one less mouth to feed.

My mother probably would've disciplined me if she'd been aware that I even had such thoughts when I was growing up. To this day, I have never told anyone in my family about these ideations, but I felt led to share this with you at this moment. I want to encourage others who may feel or have ever felt this way to know that you are not alone. If you are reading this book, then you still have an opportunity to live your life knowing that you are blessed and that there are many great reasons for you to live. Please know how important you are to your family and others.

They really care for you and about your mental, physical, and spiritual well-being.

Know that life is worth living because Jesus loves you. He was willing to die for you and your sins, as well as for the entire world. He died for those who don't even believe in, acknowledge, or trust in Him. The Holy Bible clearly states that Jesus is the way, the truth, and the life.

As I think about it, if I had ended my own life over some fifty years ago, I would've missed out on a lot of opportunities and experiences that eventually manifested in my life. I wouldn't have been here to write this book of encouragement, understanding, and support for you. I wouldn't have had my beautiful spouse, extended family, and friends. I wouldn't have been here to father, raise, and nurture the beautiful children and grandchildren with whom God has blessed me. They wouldn't have been in this world either. Now it is a scary thought to think of what I contemplated in the past to potentially affect others in the future. So how immature and selfish would I have been if I had really pursued that course of action? I wouldn't have been here to enjoy and aspire to become all that God has blessed me to become.

Yes, I am so glad that Jesus Christ had already given His life for me and my sins before I was even born. Now I know why the devil wanted to destroy me before I could realize my potential, gifts, abilities, and reasons for being alive. Life may get rough and tough at times, but at the end of the day, life is still worth living!

Never give up and never quit on life, for you didn't give yourself life and you shouldn't try to take what you didn't give yourself. You are more important than you may ever know. Please trust and believe me on this one. If you think you've got it bad, try looking around and asking others about their lives and experiences. You may be more fortunate than most. Cherish this life with which you've been blessed.

$$\sim$$

Cherish your life. This life isn't yours to take because you didn't give it.

John 3:16: "For God so loved the world that He gave His one and only Son, that whoever believes in Him shall not perish but have everlasting life."

John 10:18: "No one can take My life from me, I have the authority to give My life, and I have the authority to take My life back again."

31

Tell the Truth—
Shame the Devil

This is not a made-up story; it is all factual. I felt it was my duty from God to share my story with others. I decided not to spare anyone's feelings while revealing my truth. The unadulterated truth will set a world free if people accept the truth. Although it can be raw and unfiltered, the truth is always the best option, especially when you must sort out what's real and what's not. Secrets can be very damaging, and who do they really protect? The old saying "honesty is the best policy" isn't just a cliché. There's so much truth in that adage. They're truly words to live by.

This is the reason that many people are "sick" and many have "fallen asleep" from touching God's anointed children and prophets in attempts to do them harm. So be very humble and careful about digging a ditch for someone else, for you may be digging a ditch for yourself. There are some who hate the fact that I have had great opportunities and blessings. But my mission is to share my story with the world. Even some of my relatives and acquaintances aren't thrilled about my being able to share my humble beginnings as a way to show others how they can overcome situations that seem impossible. I just want others to know that anything's possible, especially with God's help and love.

This is a sick world full of envious, jealous, lying, devilish, sinful, evil, covetous, and backbiting people. Some even call themselves Christians and believers, but I can't tell the difference between some of them from worldly people. The Bible states that those types of people have or put on a form of godliness but deny the power thereof.

This means that they are hypocrites and liars who put on a false pretense externally, but internally are ravaging wolves and the devil's workers. Turn away from such fair-weather, deceitful people. God is not fooled and shall not be mocked. God is the Word, and the Word is the only truth that will set you free.

There are a lot of miserable people in this world. Misery really loves company. But I refuse to partake in the company of other people's misery. It's not what they eat, but what's eating them. Don't subside with miserable people, for they always have problems related to your solutions. They're equipped only with issues that you shouldn't subscribe to or take upon yourself as your problem.

Surround yourselves with people, even in your own family, who bring out the best in you and who make you feel special and important. Ignore people who discourage you because, chances are, they themselves may not have anyone in their lives to encourage them. If that's the case, seek Father God's wisdom and assurance. You will see your life unfold by leaps and bounds. You will not stagnate in doubt and unbelief. Grow from a place of freedom and deliverance from your sins. Delight yourselves in the glory of the Lord Jesus Christ.

Delight yourself in the Lord, holding onto Him until your changes come through.

Isaiah 41:10, 31:

> Fear not, for I am with you, for I am your God, I will strengthen you, I will help you, I will uphold you with my righteous right hand.

> But they who wait for the Lord shall renew their strength, they shall mount up with wings like eagles; they shall run and not be weary, they shall walk and not faint.

Job 14:14: "If a man die, shall he live again? All of my appointed times will I wait, till my changes come."

33

Liberating Souls

I really pray that my story will help some individuals in this life to know that life is not over until God says it's over. This was the beginning of my life, not the ending. I was young and didn't initially understand all that life was about. One of our biggest missions in life is to help bring truth to the people or to even learn how to tell their truths. I hope my story helps readers to find theirs without regrets or fear.

Some people will always remember my humble upbringing and how it lacked a lot of financial stability. Some of those same people want to associate me only with poverty and deprivation. They refuse to acknowledge what great things God has allowed and blessed me to become and to own. Then, there are those who, looking at me now in the present, have no clue about my past and humble beginnings. I'm living proof that God is real and able to bring you through any circumstance, no matter how bleak it looks. Be encouraged and know that we all can tell our individual stories and make them known to the world. The journey in writing this book has been very therapeutic for me. I had no clue that this would manifest as part of my calling and reason for living. I refuse to let humankind limit me or run interference with my mission and vision. While some may hide behind their pride and not expose their truths, I encourage you to rethink or at least confirm your individual purpose and reason for being.

Some of you are called to reveal your own personal experiences to help others know that, although you started from a humble place in life, Father God has and can promote you to become an effective, contributing human being in this society. At this point in time, I have realized that this journey is no longer about me, but it is about others. Operating from the gifts of help, I have been propelled with the desire to jump in and assist others in one way or another. My objective is to try to make a difference in other peoples' lives.

While I pray that this volume 1 in the succession of my life story has been an eye opener, especially for those who thought that my upbringing was ordinary, I hope it has been inspiring, offering a ray of hope. I hope it is relatable to everyday life. I will continue to encourage you in being truthful and genuine in this one natural life to live. Thank you.

A much greater place with Christ awaits us.

John 14: 1–6

> Let not your hearts be troubled. You believe in God; believe also in me. My Father's house has many rooms; if that were not so, would I have told you that I am going there to prepare a place for you? And if I go and prepare a place for you, I will come back and take you to be with me that

you also may be where I am. You know the way to the place where I am going. Thomas said to Him, "Lord, we don't know where you are going, so how can we know the way?" Jesus answered, "I am the way and the truth and the life. No one comes to the Father except through me."

Continue to be strong in the Lord and in the power of His might. Hard work still pays off, so always do your personal best to sustain and stay focused on the greatest prize. Having done all to endure, and stand, still stand.

The end of Volume 1

Printed in the United States
by Baker & Taylor Publisher Services